© NAUGHTY NOVEMBER
BY SANDEEP RAVIDUTT SHARMA

Table of Contents

Foreword IV

Naughty November...1

© NAUGHTY NOVEMBER
BY SANDEEP RAVIDUTT SHARMA

Foreword

This book provides you with a list of 100 motivational quotes and thoughts about LIFE, churned out by my mind with the divine blessings of Lord Rama and Goddess Sita. **Life is all about going forward.** Shed the baggage of the past, feed positive thoughts to your wandering mind, become the innovator by putting in the best possible efforts and keep going with a smile. Through this book, I have shared with you a bouquet of motivational and encouraging words. Let these words fill your mind with the sunshine of happiness and motivate you to live joyfully wherever you are. I'm sure if you keep reading, referring, sharing these thoughts and quotes about LIFE, you may derive inspiration and develop a good understanding of various perspectives and facts.

"The naughtiness and the innocence of a child is good enough for one to remain motivated at all times."

I sincerely hope, you will find this book amazing, interesting, rejuvenating, unique and a constant source of inspiration.

Thank You and Happy Reading.

© NAUGHTY NOVEMBER
BY SANDEEP RAVIDUTT SHARMA

© Copyright 2018 Sandeep Ravidutt Sharma - All rights reserved.
In no way is it legal to reproduce, duplicate, or transmit any part of this document in either electronic means or in printed format. Recording of this publication is strictly prohibited and any storage of this document is not allowed unless with written permission from the publisher. All rights reserved. The information provided herein is stated to be truthful and consistent, in that any liability, in terms of inattention or otherwise, by any usage or abuse of any policies, processes, or directions contained within is the solitary and utter responsibility of the recipient reader. Under no circumstances will any legal responsibility or blame be held against the author / publisher for any reparation, damages, or monetary loss due to the information herein, either directly or indirectly. The author own all copyrights.

Legal Notice:
This book is copyright protected. This is only for personal use. You cannot amend, distribute, sell, use, quote or paraphrase any part or the content within this book without the consent of the author or copyright owner. Legal action will be pursued if this is breached.

Disclaimer Notice:
Please note the information contained within this book is for motivational, educational and knowledge sharing purpose only. Every attempt has been made to provide the reader accurate, up to date and reliable complete information. No warranties of any kind are expressed or implied. Readers acknowledge that the author is not engaging in the rendering of legal, financial, medical or professional advice. By reading this document, the reader agrees that under no circumstances the author / publisher is responsible for any losses, direct or indirect, which are incurred as a result of the use of information contained within this document, including, but not limited to, —errors, omissions, or inaccuracies.

If you have further questions, contact on **Tel: +919969256731**
Email: sandeepraviduttsharma@gmail.com

© NAUGHTY NOVEMBER
BY SANDEEP RAVIDUTT SHARMA

Dedication

This book is dedicated to **Sita Ram**. Ram or Rama is one of the most important incarnation of **Lord Vishnu** while Sita or Siya is the incarnation of **Goddess Lakshmi**. Ram denotes our Soul, or the super consciousness, truth and virtue. Sita represents the ideal of feminine and spousal virtues and is known for her courage, dedication and purity. As per the ancient text of Ramayana considered sacred by people practicing Hindu religion, Lord Rama and Devi Sita are referred to as the perfect man and woman.
I hereby pray to Lord Rama and Goddess Sita, for the well being, love, happiness, strength, positive energy and success of my readers in their life. To please and evoke the powers of the Lord Rama and Mother Sita for the well being of the world, I hereby recite the following mantra...

"Sita Ram Sita Ram Sita Ram Jai Sita Ram"

NAUGHTY NOVEMBER

© NAUGHTY NOVEMBER
BY SANDEEP RAVIDUTT SHARMA

When one door closes, remember another door of opportunity gets open with the grace of the Lord.

© NAUGHTY NOVEMBER
BY SANDEEP RAVIDUTT SHARMA

The wonderful day begins with a wonderful thought.

© NAUGHTY NOVEMBER
BY SANDEEP RAVIDUTT SHARMA

The fountain of happiness flows from within.

© NAUGHTY NOVEMBER
BY SANDEEP RAVIDUTT SHARMA

Those who prepare well and attempt with confidence pass out with flying colours.

© NAUGHTY NOVEMBER
BY SANDEEP RAVIDUTT SHARMA

Life is all about maintaining a balance between beautiful lies and ugly truth.

© **NAUGHTY NOVEMBER**
BY SANDEEP RAVIDUTT SHARMA

You need to preserve valuable resource when its raining and simply stop complaining if you have failed to do so.

© NAUGHTY NOVEMBER
BY SANDEEP RAVIDUTT SHARMA

Drive in with positive thoughts and ideas and you are sure to drive out winning accolades and trophies.

© NAUGHTY NOVEMBER
BY SANDEEP RAVIDUTT SHARMA

Beautiful sights fill your mind with positive energy leading to beautiful thoughts and wonderful innovations when applied.

© NAUGHTY NOVEMBER
BY SANDEEP RAVIDUTT SHARMA

You may turn back in life for inspiration but it always prompts you to move forward.

© **NAUGHTY NOVEMBER**
BY SANDEEP RAVIDUTT SHARMA

Not by merely abstaining from work can one achieve freedom from reaction, nor by renunciation alone can one attain perfection.

© NAUGHTY NOVEMBER
BY SANDEEP RAVIDUTT SHARMA

Shaking your head can't churn out fresh thoughts. But as you enjoy the calm of your mind, it can throw million-dollar ideas at you soon.

If people listen to each other, conflicts would be no more.

Wear the ring of happiness and remember it's your efforts and mind that creates it every moment.

© **NAUGHTY NOVEMBER**
BY SANDEEP RAVIDUTT SHARMA

Break up from your past if it is pulling back your future.

© NAUGHTY NOVEMBER
BY SANDEEP RAVIDUTT SHARMA

The illusion of the path culminating into the destination keeps us moving and soon becomes reality.

Erase the depressing memories of the past by creating beautiful ones in the present.

Blend your positive thoughts with action on the ground, and you can win.

© **NAUGHTY NOVEMBER**
BY SANDEEP RAVIDUTT SHARMA

Explore your destination with a calm and curious mind.

© **NAUGHTY NOVEMBER**
BY SANDEEP RAVIDUTT SHARMA

Life gives you the option to win. It all depends on you how to use your learning to perfection and win.

The choice is available only for those who decide in time.

© NAUGHTY NOVEMBER
BY SANDEEP RAVIDUTT SHARMA

The beautiful day starts with you. Be ready to smile.

Forgetful nature is good when you are in acute pain but not when you are appearing for the test of your life.

© **NAUGHTY NOVEMBER**
BY SANDEEP RAVIDUTT SHARMA

Let your actions replicate your thoughts in the real world, and you can win.

Rise against exploitation in time or you lose the advantage to combat.

Beautiful thoughts create a wonderful world. Take the opportunity to bring them together.

Those who live on the edge hardly worry about the fall.

© NAUGHTY NOVEMBER
BY SANDEEP RAVIDUTT SHARMA

Don't lose your sincerity even if you are on the verge of losing money.

Rebuild your life this time on the foundation of good thoughts.

Be the motivation for living a joyful life.

Hold the hand of hope, and it takes you to the land of opportunities.

© NAUGHTY NOVEMBER
BY SANDEEP RAVIDUTT SHARMA

With a drop of kindness, we can fill the Ocean of humanity.

Downgrade your doubts while upgrading your self-belief if you really want to win.

Explore the world of good thoughts and make them real. Do this and you would want to repeat it again and again.

© **NAUGHTY NOVEMBER**
BY SANDEEP RAVIDUTT SHARMA

Don't let your failures contaminate your thoughts & efforts. Treat them as lessons which motivate you for the next attempt.

© **NAUGHTY NOVEMBER**
BY **SANDEEP RAVIDUTT SHARMA**

You begin your forward march by serving efforts dipped in excitement and confidence.

© **NAUGHTY NOVEMBER**
BY SANDEEP RAVIDUTT SHARMA

Good thoughts make way for the greater ones.

Look forward to meeting surprise as you move on in life.

© NAUGHTY NOVEMBER
BY SANDEEP RAVIDUTT SHARMA

Bury hatred and nurture love.

If nothing is going your way, change the way.

When you focus on your journey, the destination keeps coming closer.

© **NAUGHTY NOVEMBER**
BY **SANDEEP RAVIDUTT SHARMA**

Moments of joy spent with your near and dear ones always remain in your memory.

© **NAUGHTY NOVEMBER**
BY SANDEEP RAVIDUTT SHARMA

It is good to fight to lead when the cause is noble.

© **NAUGHTY NOVEMBER**
BY **SANDEEP RAVIDUTT SHARMA**

Fill your mind with worries of tomorrow or the joy of today. The choice is all yours.

© **NAUGHTY NOVEMBER**
BY SANDEEP RAVIDUTT SHARMA

Wild storms don't ask for anyone's permission to visit places. Have patience till they pass your door.

© NAUGHTY NOVEMBER
BY SANDEEP RAVIDUTT SHARMA

Be ready to face challenges tomorrow after you have won today.

Transform lives with your encouraging words and inspiring deeds.

© NAUGHTY NOVEMBER
BY SANDEEP RAVIDUTT SHARMA

Believe in yourself first, if you really want others to believe in you.

Revival needs complete involvement.

© **NAUGHTY NOVEMBER**
BY SANDEEP RAVIDUTT SHARMA

Dreams are good if they motivate you to make them real.

Listen to your heart before you queue up for advice.

Freedom never buys your opinion but motivates you to form it.

You may knock hundreds of doors and yet you will find the happiness within.

Not everyone has got guts to side with the Truth. Be brave.

© NAUGHTY NOVEMBER
BY SANDEEP RAVIDUTT SHARMA

Thoughts float within your mind and all around you as energy bubbles. You need to decide whether to attract, accept or reject them. Make attempt to retain good thoughts and use them to change the world for good.

Wonderful words come from a beautiful mind and a lovely heart.

© **NAUGHTY NOVEMBER**
BY SANDEEP RAVIDUTT SHARMA

PRESENT walks with you hand in hand, so why look back and ignore it now.

It's your attitude towards life which makes all the difference.

© **NAUGHTY NOVEMBER**
BY SANDEEP RAVIDUTT SHARMA

Take your decisions on time, and you can win.

Talk to resolve and not to create problems.

Confusion hardly helps, seek clarity in time.

© **NAUGHTY NOVEMBER**
BY SANDEEP RAVIDUTT SHARMA

No one would believe unless you demonstrate your capabilities in the real world.

© **NAUGHTY NOVEMBER**
BY SANDEEP RAVIDUTT SHARMA

Walk an extra mile today if you plan to relax tomorrow.

© NAUGHTY NOVEMBER
BY SANDEEP RAVIDUTT SHARMA

Why behave like a foreigner in your own country when it's time to serve your motherland.

© **NAUGHTY NOVEMBER**
BY SANDEEP RAVIDUTT SHARMA

Enrol your mind in the class of TODAY, and you know what and how to do NOW.

© NAUGHTY NOVEMBER
BY SANDEEP RAVIDUTT SHARMA

If life is a puzzle then be ready to solve it in time.

Let your efforts follow your dreams now.

Hope floats on the river of pain and sufferings.

© **NAUGHTY NOVEMBER**
BY SANDEEP RAVIDUTT SHARMA

Live wonderful moments instead of trying to save them for the future.

Step forward without any hesitation when you no longer care about the result of your actions.

© **NAUGHTY NOVEMBER**
BY SANDEEP RAVIDUTT SHARMA

The wonderful day starts with you.

© NAUGHTY NOVEMBER
BY SANDEEP RAVIDUTT SHARMA

The beautiful mountain let the water slide and form a lake on the ground. Happiness comes from sharing and giving what you have.

Don't blame others for your failure instead accept it and move again.

Pat yourself for putting in brilliant efforts even when no appreciation seems to be coming your way.

© NAUGHTY NOVEMBER
BY SANDEEP RAVIDUTT SHARMA

The amazing life is the gift of the Lord. Be thankful to him and he makes it fantastic.

© **NAUGHTY NOVEMBER**
BY SANDEEP RAVIDUTT SHARMA

Good thoughts delight the bearer.

© **NAUGHTY NOVEMBER**
BY SANDEEP RAVIDUTT SHARMA

Ring the bell if you are ready to follow the sound with full focus and attention.

© **NAUGHTY NOVEMBER**
BY SANDEEP RAVIDUTT SHARMA

Free up your mind from the stress of today, paint it up with the rainbow of good thoughts.

Whatever you plan, do things with conviction to ensure success.

© NAUGHTY NOVEMBER
BY SANDEEP RAVIDUTT SHARMA

Celebrate the festival of life each day, beginning with a beautiful smile and ending with a roar of laughter.

© NAUGHTY NOVEMBER
BY SANDEEP RAVIDUTT SHARMA

The system which discriminates should be thrown off.

© **NAUGHTY NOVEMBER**
BY SANDEEP RAVIDUTT SHARMA

Frame your golden thoughts for people to see and draw inspiration.

© **NAUGHTY NOVEMBER**
BY SANDEEP RAVIDUTT SHARMA

Be thankful to the almighty for giving you this beautiful day.

© **NAUGHTY NOVEMBER**
BY SANDEEP RAVIDUTT SHARMA

The deep thought comes from a meditative mind.

© **NAUGHTY NOVEMBER**
BY SANDEEP RAVIDUTT SHARMA

You may win against the toughest competition, but the war with your ego may take a lifetime.

© **NAUGHTY NOVEMBER**
BY SANDEEP RAVIDUTT SHARMA

Sing the song of love, and you will find joy dancing in amazement.

© **NAUGHTY NOVEMBER**
BY SANDEEP RAVIDUTT SHARMA

Think again, Is it worth to lose your patience for which you have spent years to build the same.

Challenges like your response.

© **NAUGHTY NOVEMBER**
BY SANDEEP RAVIDUTT SHARMA

We are grateful to dear Sun for bringing this day for us. Be ready to enjoy the shine.

© **NAUGHTY NOVEMBER**
BY SANDEEP RAVIDUTT SHARMA

You can afford the slide of your popularity but never ever your character.

Nothing can stop your march of prosperity if you have decided to keep going with a smile.

Transform your thoughts into action if you really want to achieve your dreams.

Be thankful to the Lord for guiding you to decide between preferring to save the life than money.

© NAUGHTY NOVEMBER
BY SANDEEP RAVIDUTT SHARMA

Beautiful words reside in a wonderful mind.

© **NAUGHTY NOVEMBER**
BY SANDEEP RAVIDUTT SHARMA

You can feel billion dollar worth of happiness just by spending a single dollar to help the other.

When you look into the eyes of the failure to understand, you can see the glimpse of the future win.

Instant thought may bring your distant dreams nearer.

It's better to drop one's selfishness, arrogance and ego in favour of humanity and kindness.

© NAUGHTY NOVEMBER
BY SANDEEP RAVIDUTT SHARMA

Your single word of motivation can do wonders.

© **NAUGHTY NOVEMBER**
BY SANDEEP RAVIDUTT SHARMA

You need to play if you want to win.

© **NAUGHTY NOVEMBER**
BY SANDEEP RAVIDUTT SHARMA

Instead of trying to shut up the world, why not surprise them by emerging as the winner.

www.ingramcontent.com/pod-product-compliance
Lightning Source LLC
Chambersburg PA
CBHW070803220526
45466CB00002B/527